The Boy Who Was Diff:

Thank

A big thank you to Mr Mansfield for inspiring me to write this. Miss Graham, Miss Cullen, Miss Crickett, Mrs Grace (SENCO), Miss McDonald, Gail Jessop, Mrs Stephenson, Mrs Grace (Form teacher), Miss Lindop, Mrs Holmes, Mrs Price and of course my wonderful family.

Especially my amazing Mum!

Thank you all!!

Part 1:

There was once a boy named Jude, who had a pretty hard life. He looked like an ordinary person, but he wasn't. He was someone who was very special. He was loved very much. Jude knew that because he could tell how his Mum and Dad treated him.

One day he found out that he had been diagnosed with Asperger's. From that day onwards, it changed his whole life completely. Everything started to change for Jude, he was too scared to come out of the house encase something happened, or if he forgot to lock the door on the way out.

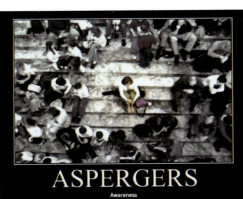

As his life carried on, he started to get angrier and angrier every time he had an argument. Jude kept on getting more and more

The Boy Who Was Different - Daniel Hinnigan

stressed every day. After school he would go straight to his room and think about himself or go on his laptop to calm down. There was something special about Jude; it was that he could remember everything he had done. His nickname from his family was Rain man. Jude never got it. He thought to himself, is this joke or are they being mean? He never had a clue.

The Boy Who Was Different - Daniel Hinnigan

Jude was very emotional. Sometimes, he was too scared to let his feelings out encase someone said something mean to him. When Jude came to the end of Year 6, he was even more stressed out. The reason for this is because; he was scared for Secondary School. He kept on crying and getting angrier until the point where he had to talk about his feelings, even though it upset him when he talked about them. He got told how to cope with stress and anger. So he got some tips for it, he looked at them all the time. They helped him in difficult situations. Jude had started Secondary School, he found it tough. He got bullied, he wasn't very happy. Suddenly it got to the point where he didn't want to come to school anymore. But he had to, so he had to cope with it. After about two months, the bullying had stopped. He felt very happy to get it off his chest. He found the work and the homework hard, but he got through it.

He always gave up before he had started it or tried it. He wanted to understand his work, so he done extra work at home, it helped him, he kept on doing it and doing it. He pushed himself to be confident about his work, so did his teachers.

At the end of school, as he got

home, he used to think for ages or just look at random things and think about them. He always searched up facts about Asperger's or read books about it. It made him upset, really upset, but he talked about the facts and the books. Jude realised, as he was getting older, he wanted to have a career in music.

So the pieces of the puzzle are starting to fit together. Or were they...

The Boy Who Was Different

As time goes by...

Part 2:

Yes the pieces of the puzzle were starting to fit together. For a little while anyway.

Just until Jude had got used to his new experience, the pieces all fell apart. Jude just couldn't cope with school anymore. Even after all the bullying had stopped.

But the bullying had started again then stopping, then coming back. But Jude had gotten used to the fact that he just had to be brave and toughen up a little.

In the May of year 7, Jude had agreed with his mum to start getting the bus to school. Jude had always been the early bird of the family, getting up

The Boy Who Was Different - Daniel Hinnigan

between 4 and 5 in the morning.

So can you now imagine what time he would be leaving the house and the time getting into school?

So yes, if you said leaving the house at 7 and getting into school at 8, then you were right!

Jude like getting the bus to school of a morning and getting it home as well. He enjoyed this because he could

The Boy Who Was Different - Daniel Hinnigan

be trusted to do his own thing for once.

Now Jude had gotten through and survived Year 7. Now it was time for Year 8...

In the last week of the summer holidays, Jude was thinking about Year 8 and thinking of all the changes.

The Boy Who Was Different – Daniel Hinnigan

Jude hates changes. Whenever his routine changes he gets emotional and vulnerable, then starts to get a little angry.

When Jude was thinking about Year 8, he started to sweat and start lashing out at his family. Then he started crying.

After a couple of months in Year 8, Jude had finally gotten used to it by now. Especially all of the changes.

The Boy Who Was Different – Daniel Hinnigan

Time was going fast for Jude. He liked it because then his school week would be over. But then here came the homework. It got too much for Jude and he was embarrassed that he couldn't cope with all of the homework.

But then the weekend ended. This meant he had to go back to school. This is what he dreaded, every Sunday!

The Boy Who Was Different - Daniel Hinnigan

Jude was getting bullied again. But this time it was a lot more different. He was getting pushed around, getting called names and even people were kicking his chair in lessons.

He didn't know what to do. Does he tell someone? Does he stand up for himself? Or does he just keep it too himself and bottle it all up?

Well, he bottled it all up and didn't tell anyone.

The Boy Who Was Different - Daniel Hinnigan

Until it reached breaking point...

- Jude's Asperger syndrome label was really annoying him. The feeling of him being labelled by some person who doesn't know the full Jude was getting to him emotionally.

The Boy Who Was Different – Daniel Hinnigan

Jude wondered that if he didn't have Asperger's, would he be getting bullied, would he feel that he wouldn't want to come to school if he didn't have it.

He was thinking and thinking of what to do. Jude didn't have many friends because he didn't know how to communicate with other people. So he struggled.

Jude was really stressed by now. He didn't know what

The Boy Who Was Different – Daniel Hinnigan

to do. He went to the SENCO and had a chat with her. He also spoke to his councillor and discussed the issue with her.

Jude was asked if he was having any problems at home. He didn't.

That was then. After a few weeks had passed, Jude was having problems at home.

He thought

that everything was going downhill.

His dad was splitting up with his wife and they were possibly going their separate ways. This turned Jude's world upside-down completely.

Jude was coming up with plans to get his Dad and his wife back together. Just too even talk or even to make eye-contact. But nothing worked.

But after a while, they got back together.

The Boy Who Was Different - Daniel Hinnigan

So after a long period of time. They saw some sense in each other.

But after everything went great again, something terrible happened...

One of Jude's favourite people had passed away. Val was like a Nan to him. He used to call her Ninny Val. She had dementia for four years. But he was happy that she wasn't in pain anymore. He could hold it together at home, but when he came to school, he was really upset.

The Boy Who Was Different - Daniel Hinnigan

He felt really guilty because he felt like he was having a great time and everyone was sad at home because he was on a school trip.

Jude will probably never get over it, he will still always get upset, but he knows that she isn't in pain anymore and that it's best for her.

But about the bullies, he will just ignore them and get on with his own life. And to not worry about them. He had now realised that the bullying will just keep coming back. But it is tough for the people who want everyone to be the same because it will never happen.

But people with Asperger's aren't weird. We are gifted!

So it does look like the pieces of the

The Boy Who Was Different - Daniel Hinnigan

puzzle are definitely
starting to fit together...

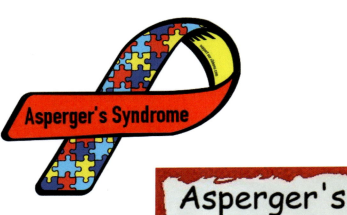

Author:
Daniel Hinnigan

The Boy Who Was Different – Daniel Hinnigan

Daniel Joseph Hinnigan is from Liverpool, England. He was born in 2002. He has Asperger syndrome and Jude is based upon him.  He went to a private nursery in Allerton called Bluebird. He then went onto Primary school to Our Lady of Good Help in Wavertree. He left there in Year 6 and was educated and still is here at Saint Francis Xavier's College Woolton.

Printed in Great Britain
by Amazon